MW01608661

*w **h i s p e r*** from the shadows

poetry by Har'i Khan

TATE PUBLISHING, LLC

whisper from the shadows

Torment Burning Cold

What is the torment burning cold
With the moments that we stole
In the night of dreams and passion bold
The bed sheets together we unfold

Now I sit in chamber blind
Your image my last dream enshrined
In a room cold and silken lined
The past a place I'll never find

I sit now deaf and listen to the rain
Holding tight to the nightmare's mane
I wish away your image of joyous pain
And now on my heart a lasting stain

Was it just a fantasy in the night
I now stand torn in the void of your sight
And wander in the dark without your light
To never hold the illusion again, a chilling fright

What is the torment burning cold
With the moments that we stole
In the night of dreams and passion bold
The bed sheets together we unfold

The Idealist

In a vision once I had
I crossed the ocean twice too far
I set on the shore of an ancient sea
I watched the ships sink, one, two, and three

I dared to ask of questions, why
I found myself aloft, as I could fly
I searched the hills and valleys there
I almost paid the toll, the final fare

I walked with death as we talked of life
I thought of sanity as I took his sister as my
wife
I moved away boulders to look under rocks
I found the keys to a thousand locks

I saw cities in the sky and dammed nations on
earth
I witnessed the loss of life in the miracle of
birth
I dined with kings and slept with vagrants
I dressed in rags I wore with elegence

So here I stand a day later

Looking at a journey only destiny could cater
Now I close my eyes at last
Now from dreams am I cast

In a vision once I had
I heard the children fall
I took the hands of demons in flight
I touched the eye of god and saw endless night

Silken Black Bird

The raven perched upon the shoulder of a boy who tries to become a man. A man of strife and power, but yet humble and silent. Sent by those who used to lead kings in their rule of empires. Who used to fly on dragon's back and sit among the stars. Who used to walk with saints and show the people lights long since forgotten. Lights that no one would have ever seen though never had they brightened nor have they faded. Just not to be seen by those who don't look. Now the boy tries to be their rebirth. All that is wanted is to reach out and help mortal man live on. Without their guidance man has befallen the wrath of the gods and if not shone glitter again shall fall to the pits of hell.

The raven whispers secrets long forgotten to the lad of chosen fate. Secrets once buried with wizards and sorcerer long sins past.

> To fly on dragon's back
> To sit among the stars
> To hold a flicker of flame

The raven whispers secrets long forgot, but will he stand forward of kings before the empire falls?.... ...

Look for the Shore

I search for the shore
  In vainness of the darken day
  looking as I fight for air

I search for the shore
  The sharks circle as I fight the waves
  looking as I fall beneath the water's edge

I search for the shore
  My arms tire as they bleed
  looking for a light darkened by a cloak

I search for the shore
  as leeches suckle my flesh in lust
  looking to land I search

I find the shore but do not feel the ground
  As tentacles pull at me
  looking in vain for I can not see

I find the shore but do not feel the ground
  My skin is soaked and dripping sweat
  looking for what I found

I turn back to the water

and fall to my nurturing leeches
like a "lion in winter"

Mariah

I sit to wait for her
    she does not come
I listen and wait for her
    she does not come

As her whisper comes not on the wind
    her gentle knock comes not at my door
    her subtle kiss meets not my lips

I watch and wait for her
    she does not come
I feel and wait for her
    she does not come

As the warmth of her soothing touch
    the softness of her silken flesh
    the sweetness of her embracing smile

I wish and wait for her
    she does not come
I dream and wait for her
    she does not come

As she is not a whisper to carry upon the wind

she is not a fantasy lost in the twisting wind
she is nothing but the wind's own breath as
it caresses past in one fleeting flurry
as once here she is now gone

My Three Loves

Desire

I was three hours twenty minutes
    into the future
        And there I met your frightened touch
        Even though ours was a loving touch

I was three hours twenty minutes
    into the future
        And there I found you alone
        But always your past to your side

I was three hours twenty minutes
    into the future
        And there we fell to each other
        scared of what we wanted - but wanting
        it all

I was three hours twenty minutes
    into the future
        And there we met to find
        how alone we really were

You always with your lover

trying to get away
but afraid to turn to me

You always with your lover
And you embraced me
But the grasp stifled your love

You always with your lover
We wished to feel our love
But the fear held us apart

You always with your lover
And from him you tried to turn
And for that you could not let yourself
love me

I had to leave
for I was not knowing where I was
But it was so well I knew

I had to leave
And so I turned back to what I run from
And so I turn my back to what I run to

I had to leave
So the plug was pulled and the clock stopped
So the plug is pulled and time goes on

I had to leave
And now I am cursed for I fear to never find
my way back

And now you travel within my memory

Curse the fates for in fear I left
 what I had looked for
 so long and I may not be
 able to get back but
 I shall always remember
 That fear kept me from
 the one I desired without
 lust
  May you find the
  love of a soul without
   flesh

Fear

I was three hours twenty minutes
 into the future
  And there I felt my emotions touch
  my soul and more, to see the light

I was three hours twenty minutes
 into the future
  And there I found myself alone
  But always my fears to my side

I was three hours twenty minutes
 into the future
  And there we fell to each other
  Not knowing what was there - I saw it all

I was three hours twenty minutes
    into the future
        And there we met to find
        how alone we really were

You always with your lover
    Tearing you away from your life
        And for that I embrace you
        You always with your lover

And he held us both in his bonds
    And the grasp almost pulled us under
        You always with your lover
        Our love stifled

And we nearly fell
    You always with your lover
        And to it you must turn
        And for that you shall be free of it

I had to leave
    For I was not knowing where I was
        But it was so well I knew

I had to leave
    And so I turned back to what I run from
        And so I turned my back to what I run to

I had to leave
    So the plug was pulled and the clock stopped
        So the plug is pulled and time goes on

I had to leave
  And now I am cursed for I fear to never find
    my way back
      And now you travel within my
      memory

Curse the fates for there
  I was blinded and could not
  hear the voices tell
  of the truth in faces
  of belief for now I
  left the time I was
  free and return to my
  shackles
    But I shall fly
  upon dragon's wings
  my sword sharpened

Intellect

I was three hours twenty minutes
  into the future
    And there I met your fascinated touch
      though our embrace was apart

I was three hours twenty minutes
  into the future
    And there I found you alone
      but your destiny to your side

I was three hours twenty minutes
    into the future
        And there we fell to each other
         Prophesizing the past - worried
        about the future

I was three hours twenty minutes
    into the future
        And there we met to find how
        alone we really were

You always with your lover
    Bound in embrace of endless lust
        and in that lust I found you

You always with your lover
    And in your embrace I was engulfed
        but found only pieces of myself

You always with your lover
    Afraid to show our love to each other
        Those about us knew its strength

You always with your lover
    And to it you will always be bound
        And for that I shall be bound to you

I had to leave
    For I was not knowing where I was
        But it was so well I knew

I had to leave
    And so I turned back to what I run from
        And so I turn my back to what I run to

I had to leave
    So that plug was pulled and the clock
stopped
        So the plug is pulled and time goes on

I had to leave
    And now I am cursed for I fear to never find
      my way back
      And now you travel with my memory

Curse the fates for in your
    grasp I am cradled like
    the student that teaches
    the master and now my
    worries are of my return
    to the future where I
    left you held in my
    grasp though we never embraced
        The poets rebel pen
        is stronger than any sword

Spiritual

I was three hours twenty minutes
    into the future
        And there I met your loving touch
       though we never embraced

I was three hours twenty minutes
    into the future
        And there I found you alone
       but always your love to your side

I was three hour twenty minutes
    into the future
        And there we fell to each other
       looking for something - when we had
       all

I was three hours twenty minutes
    into the future
        And there we met to find how
       alone we really were

You always with your lover
    And for that I fell in love with you
       And wished to hold you tight

You always with your lover
    And he too wished to embrace me
       But never shall you understand why

You always with your lover
    Even as we made love
      in an unconsummated affair

You always with your lover
    And from him you shall not turn
      And for that I fell in love with you

I had to leave
    for I was not knowing where I was
      But it was so well I knew

I had to leave
    And so I turned back to what I run from
      And so I turn my back to what I run to

I had to leave
    So the plug was pulled and the clock stopped
      So the plug is pulled and time goes on

I had to leave
    And now I am cursed for I fear to never find
    my way back
      And now you travel within my memory

Curse the fates for it is not
    Till I left that I knew
    where I was and now I can
    only pray that I will find
    my way back to the future
      But here a tear shall I

drop for you and with it
I know you can make steps
to heaven

Journey

I took a journey, I do not remember
    "There are too many roads"

I walked a path, trotted bear
    through a desert of souls

I walked beneath the limbs of trees
    that never grow

The first thing I never met
    was an old man that wasn't there
    playing in an empty field
    his laughter was silent in the
          rain

The second thing I never met
    was a hare sitting at a table
    with a tortoise and a lamb, eating
    pork and spinach
The hare asked me
    "What didn't the old man say as
    I passed?"
I answered him with silence then
    turned away to leave that

place I never was

The third thing I don't remember
    was a wolf tap-dancing with seven
    chorus girls wearing green two-twos
       He never told me the tale of
       the four nuns and a camel

The fourth thing I never left
    was the first thing I never met
    as he sat across the table from
    me . . .
       I wept

I took a journey, I do not remember
    "There were too many roads"

A Table Away

She sat there just a table away
    no one I knew, no identity
    just there, a table away

Like me she seamed to be waiting
    waiting for someone
    someone we both wait for
    someone that will never come

I watch her sitting just a table away
    silent and to herself
    I think about approaching her
    talking quietly, maybe a smile
        a polite nod. . . . I didn't

I watch her sitting there, just a table away
    watching, waiting, thinking
    she sits there
    was she thinking the same
    did she want the conversation
        If I wait will she approach me

I wait as she sits there just a table away
    no name just an idea I'll always remember

Like me she appears to be waiting
    for someone that will never show
    someone we both wait for . . .

And as I ride away and we share a final
glance I ask myself if I would recognize the
person I wait for or would she recognize me?

Concrete & Steel

They walk a path
of fright and fear
They walk a path
of flowing tear

Their tall thin bodies
sway with the breeze
Their tiny corpses
walk without ease

There shone the light
to guide their way
And then by lies
they're told what to say

They walk a path
of concrete and steel
and showed the world
so far from real

Their feet are swallowed
by earth and mud
Held fast to drowned
in a material flood

Their vision blinded
by their TV guide
as in their dens
they set to hide

Alone they're surrounded
by peering sound
Their empty dreams
a vacant mound

They are the children
of concrete and steel
all they know is
the final meal

A prayer for peace
A hope for light
An empty shadow
locks them in night

VCRs shall play
their past
As again and again
they'll see it last

A sight of tomorrow
held so dear
a guiding voice
To steer them clear

They are the children

of concrete and steel
all they know
is so far from real

Video games
let them play war
while in their fear
it's a festering whore

Tomorrow for them
a day at the mall
Their world keeps them
locked in the hall

Their time
may be lost
as to them
all is tossed

The scraps of
our hate
which is their
tomorrow's debate

The bomb we built
from our own steel
The walls we built
all just too real

For they are the children
of concrete and steel

They are our tomorrow
ALL SO REAL!

Why

I sit scared, lonely, sad and tired
I set scared of the future, for I do not know
what to employ for what it brings.
Scared of the loss of what I leave, to return to
someday, for they may not be there when I return
from my voyages.
Scared that I may not know when the voyage has
reached the end.
(To be scared: to sit in hope for
what you are not sure.)

I sit lonely for though there are friends to truly
befriend me they never truly know what is within
me.
Lonely for I yearn for the company of those I had
left to past, and who's trails led away from mine.
Lonely to hold the flesh of women that will
still be there after the sun has dawned.
(To be lonely: to sit blind to the
sights of others for they sit

blinded to the sights of your mind.)

I sit sad for the pain that fills my heart, the
heart that finds it hard to beat a steady rhythm as
it bleeds to be heard.
Sad for I call to those who will never hear my
voice, and stride away from my presence, unable to
stop.
(To be sad: to loose what you once
held and since you once held it you
know the void it has left.)

I sit tired for the road has worn me and I still
have so much to travel.
Tired for I have seen, and I have heard, and I
have felt so much. . . . but yet I know I have more
still to see and hear and feel. . . .
(To be tired: to look back and see
the cluttered road behind you, to
look ahead and see the cluttered
road in front of you.)

Night's Tranquility

To sway the night's tranquility
    in vivid colors white
    and make the pearl black
    and wish away the fright
    I held an undine in my grasp
    a maiden soul of pleasure lust
    and love gone to flutter by
    I held the love I grasp

To sway the night's tranquility
    tied to colors bright
    and in the blue of the bay
    a moon lit night to stray
    the coming ship, a lost hope
    a maiden set upon a stone
    as if it were her very throne

There in the harbor I cry
    as the maiden sang her lullaby
    I sway from my post,
    to fear the great ship lost
        "To stern - to stern!"

the mighty vessel toss
and I no longer saw the maiden
as the vessel rolled to bay
her song shallows my memory forever
as to land I never made
and in the drink I set lost
with the vessel who's captain
still is heard as the harbor floor is disbursed
"To stern - to stern!"

To sway the night's tranquility
the colors of the night
as here with ocean in my sight
I dream a dream of land
turned over in the night
as a hundred men sink fast in
frigid fright

I saw the maiden on a stone
I heard her song within the air
to demon she did sing
and sang the ship a scare
that left a hundred men to
till the mast
a chore forever to last
A hundred men now rot at sea
because a maiden sang her song to me

To sway the night's tranquility
    the color is of fright
    a peril's steel, the ivory side
    a hundred men lie in the tide
    I look about their restless souls
    as at me they look in pain
    as within their glare
    they question me insane

For I saw the maiden upon the stone
    as now her demon I have grown
    as a hundred men now round my grave
    to say I dug theirs one by one
    as now the darkness of the sun
    shines where the deed was done

For in the night's tranquility
    when you listen hard and long
    you'll hear the maiden's song
    that toppled the vessel that rolled to bay
    in the light of a darkened day
    as sung by the maid
    for her lover lost to sea
    I've heard this song sung to me
    once in the night's tranquility

In Your Eyes

In your eyes I see eternity's blink
In your eyes I find an eternal link
In your eyes I feel myself sink

With you my joy flows with grace
with you my life finds its pace
with you I burst free from my case

> I feel my will naked in the rain
> I feel my grief is fought and slain
> I feel your touch and pull away from all
> insane

>> My freedom in your hand I feel
>> My freedom in your heart I heal
>> My freedom in your love I seal
>> My freedom in your eyes I see all
>> so real

The Poet's Pen

Am I but not a poet's ink
    flowing from the quill
    to cover a sheet of
    ivory canvas in tale

Am I not the writer's quill
    falling to fill the gap
    between the hand
    and the paper beneath

Could it be my creator is but
    a writer telling the tale of
    a life, letters drawing pictures
    and pictures giving me breath

Am I the sum of a pen
    the ink my life
    the paper my world
    the writer my god

And in the turn of a page
Am I but a memory in some
    stranger's mind, for I

shall be folded and
put away the night
and in dreams tell of a world
that I have created and on
the waking dawn I shall
write of a person in my pen
and my ink shall draw his portrait
and my paper shall be his world
and he shall tell of
     his ink
     and his pen
     and his world

We all are created by our god's image
     and
We all have created our god's image

Seasons

To the winter's breath
    A cold calling of the night
I see the maiden waiting by the pool
    for her lover
she has called again and again
she has listened again and again
she has waited again and again

To the spring's breath
    a cold calling of the night
I see the pool swelling by the maiden
    waiting for her lover
its dark red waves ripple again and again
its dark red waves wash again and again
its dark red waves waiting again and again

To the summer's breath
    a cold calling of the night
I see the maiden by the pool
    both waiting for their lovers
her brilliant white robe drops to the ground

her pearl flesh pales to the moon's glow
as she steps forth to the pool

To the autumn's breath
    a cold calling of the night
I see the pool swelling about the maiden
    who has met her lover there
its dark red waves part to hold her
as it engulfs her silken flesh
embracing her as she vanishes from sight

To woo the maiden beauty
    silken flesh of pearl white
        and love to share the moon lit
        night

The Empty Room

As I step forth
    into an empty room
Full of people
    that show no gloom

They walked about
    like mourners they'd sing
And I heard them talk
    of many a thing

Their empty hands
    held glasses of wine
As they strolled about
    to talk and dine

And to air
    played a band
That at the far of the room
    I saw them stand

A waltz as light
    as a cotton blouse
So cheerful was the mood

of the empty house
But as I wade
    through the room
I felt a draft
    As if I stood in my tomb

And away went each
    little form
As if caught
    in its own little storm

The wind swept silent
    as it brushed by my side
And I now felt cold
    as if stripped of my hide

And then
    on a marble throne
Set a figure
    made of stone

As I looked
    to me he turned
Then a flame in his eyes
    leapt up to burn

He was a little form
    all hunched and green
I came to see an imp
    set in the scene

A chuckley voice
    rose from his chin
And before I could speak
    the room started to spin

Then again I stood
    posed at the door
But this time in the room
    beckoned a whore

Her silken black flesh
    was scarred by a whip
As she held out a glass
    and told me to sip

Though her voice was mute
    to my naked ears
I drank of the glass
    that was filled with her tears

They were sweet
    to my tongue
but in me they stood
    and they stung

Then she backed
    out of my reach
And took a bite
    of a luscious peach

Her swirling hair

coiled and twisted
As I watched
my vision was misted

When it cleared
again the room was full
With dancing figures
that danced around a bull

A scarlet beast
with three massive heads
All ten of its eyes
were all shades of reds

It stood so still
as they danced around
As if a secret of the beast
wanted to be found

Then the whore
took my hand
And before the bull
I was now to stand

Its breath reeked
of whiskey and beer
As it stood on the corpse
of a small baby deer

It rutted the floor
and grunted my name

Walked around me twice
 and said I was the blame

Then the music did still
 and all turned to me
Then they turned away
 and wandered cross the sea

So again the room
 stood still
And I and my shadow
 were all left to fill

So I set to wait
 but my shadow stood to pace
Then walked to a corner
 where it opened a case

Then pulled out a suit
 of colors so bright
The room was lit
 by a rainbow of light

And again stood a throne
 of glittering pearl
And upon it set
 a very young girl

She wore a silken
 white dress
And in her right hand

she held a press
She filled it with
    the pages of a book
Then from beneath
    a golden chalice she took

She handed it to me
    and smiled so queer
As I look to the chalice
    with a bit of a leer

It was filled with blood
    up to the brim
and in it I saw
    I was trying to swim

Then with a giggle
    and a sweet little kiss
The girl was gone
    like some forgotten bliss

The light grew dim
    and the room more clear
As for the door
    I turned to steer

But there stood
    the three-headed bull
As around his neck
    he wore a fur stole

It charged at me
    with thrust to kill
As I stood in its path
    frighten and still

But it came to a halt
    and looked me square
Then vanished with
    a most elegant flair

So I walked
    to the door
I walked right
    past the whore

As she stepped
    into reach
And offered a bite
    of her luscious peach

As I took hold
    of the knob
I heard the imp
    as he started to sob

The music again
    started to play
As I opened the door
    and walked into the day

A House in Madness

A house in madness we built
    on a hill that has no tilt
A dream of golden steeds to ride
    in madness we come to hide

I look into the garden
    begging a sparrow's pardon
I see her sitting naked with fairies
    as the melody of the breeze does carry
    all so gentle and merry

I stand on the porch
    to write in the light of a torch
my words fall short with your grace
    as I see you knelt by the fairies in lace
    your form . . . they fly around in trace

We step into the gentle caress of the pool
The day's dew washed away by the waters . . .
so cool
I taste your supple lips, and take your hand
    as now we find in paradox we land
    and the fairies lay (a sprite full band)

I touch your silken side
    my soul and heart with you shall subside
As we sit on the bow of the house so warm
    we sit so quiet in our silken dorm
      safe from the battles of the raging storm . . .

Here in the house that madness built
    on a hill that has no tilt
A dream of golden steeds to ride
    in madness we come to hide
      deep . . . deep . . . inside

Her Eyes

Her eyes
    such subtle pools of light
As she looks into
    the still of the night

Setting on the banister
    awaiting a gentle call
As from her fingers
    a rose does fall

In her hand
    she holds a mirror
As within
    lays a stolen tear

The candles that
    light her dorm
Waver slightly
    as they become the storm

The tables and chairs
    are an emerald white
The silken sheets of her bed
    are pulled so tight

As she sits
    on her balcony
Watching the night
    like some endless sea

The harvest moon
    lights the yard
From which her love
    could never be barred

Then a hawk
    circles the air
Then lands at her side
    with such gentle care

She looks to its eyes
    and strokes its back
As it sets by her hand
    a satin sack

She smiles
    as from within
She draws a string
    spun from tin

And then a vial
    of scarlet pearl
Which wrapped with the string
    starts to twirl

She closes her eyes

and speaks out in threes
A word she hears echoed
   in the branches of the trees

And then to turn
   in a circle twice
To find herself
   in a cavern of ice

Where stood a form
   both bold and stern
For this is the one
   to which she does turn

A welcoming embrace
   so tight does he hold
The woman for which
   the night he stole

The crystal walls
   hold tight their secret
As in these caverns
   they both are met

In loving embrace
   of a moment lent
Then sounds of love
   to the gods are sent

But the eve with dawn
   grows late

and all now is met
	by the hand of fate

She turns to look
	sadly away
And finds the light
	of an unwelcome day

As it shines on her
	at her window sill
And all the morning
	hold so still

As she closes
	the silent mirror
That holds a pale
	and faded tear

And turns to walk
	into her room
Where she'll set
	to wait in solemn gloom

For comes the next
	harvest moon
All sets in stride
	of an ancient tune

As she waits
	As she waits
		As she waits

Wedding Bells

I look
I listen
    I hear the singing of the bells
        as they reach out
        and to all they tell
            of the dance
            within the hall
    But suddenly I feel the pain
    of my last beat
        to stall

I listen
I look
    to see in maiden's bridal white
        The image I fear, and turn away
        to hide deep in my night
    Set at my window's pane
        I drop a tear
        hidden by the rain

I look
I listen
    I hear the tale in song
        Of every sound to air
           for which I long
    But here I set to know
        that which never was
           away with the wind, does blow
    A wagered dream, of silent mist
        all to vanish,
           with an unseen twist

I look
I listen
    I hear the voices as they are spoke
        and within I stand to die
           as empty, my heart is broke
           like a crystal glass
               by a subtle rose
    Take from its roots
    so never more it grow

I look
I listen
    I hear the laughter of a silent cry
        The fall of a wish
           on the thorns I lie

and listen to the story
    I hear in the tell
    as I listen to the sound
    of the wedding bell . . .

A Man of Ages Many

I

I met a man
   of ages many
That talked of time ago
   in a place of beauty plenty

"Where is the place
   of which you speak?"
Asked I
   in a question of youth

II

I met a man
   of ages many
He told me
   of love's vast throne

"A chair of crystal
upon he set
   with
diamonds and incense
silver and gold"

This he said
    with a strangled voice
        so he asked
    of a glass of wine

"May I of your
    nectar drink
        to quench my thirst?"

Then with a nod
    he drank of it

III

I met a man
    of ages many
He told of the table
    by which love set

"A spread of feast
    vast it was
    to fill the appetite
        of any and many a man"

I met a man
    of ages many

Then upon a loaf
    of bread
He cast his stare
    and then he asked of it

"May I slice?
of your kneaded dough
to quench my hunger?"

Then with a nod
    he ate of the loaf

And I looked
    to him
and I asked again
    of him

       "Where is this place
       of which you speak?"

    IV

I met a man
    of ages many
That had a tale to tell
    and it be he
       spoke of a land he saw

And he told
    of love's own throne of crystal
Upon he set with
    diamonds and incense
silver and gold
and
of his table

long and bold
On which there set a feast
   to feed every
      and many a man

And then he looked
   to me again
and these last words he spoke

   "And when I blinked
   the table was bare
   the jewels were gone
   but love still set
   There upon his throne
   still strong and bold
   as he always was"

   V

I buried a man
   Of ages many
And upon the marker
   I bare these words

   "Where is this place
   of which you speak?"

How Fragile is our Time

How fragile is our time
  together in the twist of night
  I sit and wish to hold you
  in my embrace so tight

How fragile is our time
  every minute is a gem
  our lives thorned like
  the rose's slender stem

How fragile is our time
  as taken in quick stride
  we find in the past
  where we turn to hide

How fragile is every minute
  we have each other's embrace
  as we stand together
  in a room face to face

The very twilight of our
  fragile hopes and pleas
  The night to come all to fast

and we watch as it flees
And again I ask
How fragile is our time
together in the twist of night
we sit and hold our embrace
so tight

Epigram

If to a single room
I shall be locked
Make it an attic
with but a single window
faced to the heart
of humanity
As so I may call out
my love

Scarlet Dove

I hold tight the scarlet dove
    as its cold black feathers
        burn my hand
I cry a tear of ice
    as on the desert shore I stand

    My night comes cold
    with an empty stare
    The dove I hold
    is my day's despair

    Where do I go now?
    Where do I go from here?
    What is the cloak I wear
    in my dream of fear

    The dove turns and plucks out my eye
    then full of madness it stops to cry
    A long and cold silent song
    sung of the maiden
        her story so long

No time lay empty

in stark we lay cold
The day grows late
the sun grows old

We quest to sleep
and dream of the day
But in our night
the dove has come to stay

The Apology

My dearest love:

In time hast past I have felt heavy a burning upon my heart. For I could not have known, but did.

Yes I remember the time we had, the way you waited for me time and time again. The faithfulness you showed, the trust. And yet I turned on you without understanding what I had done.

Yes I remember when first we met, you lost and strayed brought to me in rags. I gave you shelter and warmth , you repaid with love. So often I wish we were of the same kind, but that could not be. And yet I turned on thee without understanding what I had done.

Yes I remember when you set waiting for my return, you set by my heart, you would run to me when I entered and walk with me when I left. You trusted me to fault, and yet I turned on thee without understanding what I had done.

Yes, I remember when you let her into my life, you were patient and understanding. And as we got further apart you waited patient and understanding. And when I left you sitting there alone. . . . . you died of a broken heart.

So now I write, for now I know
"I turned on you with understanding what I had done"

I apologize all too late . . . all to weak

With love,

What Child is This

What child is this I stand to see
that stands so still to look at me
What child is this I dare not flee
that stands so still to look at me

I hear its tears as they dampen the floor
I stare in the hollow of its mind's last store
and hear the whisper of its pain all the more
I hear its tears as they dampen the floor

What child is this I stand to see
that stands so still to stare at me
What child is this I dare not flee
that stands so still to stare at me

As I hear its tiny cry fall still
as it is an ear shattering shrill
To scrape through my spine a deathly chill
as I hear its tiny cry fall still

Who is this child I listen to cry
Who is this child I watch fall and die
Who is this child I leave to lie

What child is this I watch fall and die

From where does it come in such joyless pain
for what does it stand in sorrow's reign
Who is this child that death shall ordain
from where does it come in such joyless pain

The child I lay in the earth to rest
and put on its stone an immortal crest
I look to the child with dirt on its chest
the child I lay in the earth to rest

The sign of the phoenix cut so bold
to tell the story without end once it's told
For from the grave I turn to leave
the side of the grave where I stood to grieve

What child is this I stand to see
that stands so still to look at me
What child is this I dare not flee
that stands so still to look at me. . . . .

Song of Distants

Distant land to a far
like sparrows voices carry
upon the wind of hope and prayer
across a void I listen

Distant land to a far
like spring time breeze through reed
upon the tide of lost despair
across a void I listen

Distant land to a far
like crickets dance on moon lit lakes
upon air of lighted bays
across a void I listen

Wonderment falls my soul
desire fills my breast
to dream a picture of the song
that fills the air and rides the wind
that comes upon the tide from
Distant lands to a far
across a void
I listen . . . .

Fingers Dance

About the threads of fate
about the threads of time
about the threads of lost and gained
Dance the fingers to and through
run about and scream and shout
Upon the threads dainty and fine dance
the fingers and dance so fine allure
of pleasure and care of freedom
joy of tenderness all in time
    Upon the threads of fate and time
    upon the threads of love and care
    upon the threads dance on and on the
    fingers
The fingers dainty and fine in rhythm in space
to gods in haste pleasure in tenderness
Love in shape an unwanted heart
to dance upon the threads of space and time
and care of touch so gentle upon the threads
The threads dance on
upon the threads dance on and on

oh fingers so delicate dance upon
the threads
Dance on . . .

The Hunger of the Tree

The tree stands
its roots stretched out
and plunged into
the blood stained sands

The crust of the soil
hardened
as in the sight of
two suns
there lay no pardon

Its age in decadences
its rotting aroma
arrogant
filling the air with
a whoring scent

Behind it set
the Black Hills
shadow of white
the crevices fill

The sky darkened
as two suns glare
a cold dead stare

As the lost and weary
in its tentacles
are buried
and there souls
immortally married

Its tentacles hunger
for the mortal flesh
which in lust
they tear to a mesh

The six heads
hover over
the ever-resting beds
Looking for the lost
child
and in a voice ever so
mild

It calls to them
it turns to them
it devourers them

To feed its branches

as their jaws
strike like lances
as the suns look down
in glances

Their darken sight
luminous to the night

And behold
the six-sided pyramid
streaks to the sky
as in the center
of the tree
it does hide

And about its peek
the vision
shall the weary seek

For their dances
the yellow winged
serpent

And in his sight
is the image the weary
hold tight

For it is the snake

of air
to quest your
stare

As the tale holds
the vision sight
as it is
the all-seeing eye
it holds tight

So quest the beast
and feed the tree
a feast

As to now
the future is come
and beat the drum

For the dawn
is won by night
and there it is
in dusk's sight

So shall the journey
be taken
is it worth the feast
you're making

Or shall we just turn
and leave it be
for when tomorrow comes
it will be with the rise
of the suns

The enchanted destiny
the enchanted ebony
of a new day be brought
by the suns to us
be taught

The new is the new
and
the old is the old
and there is no need
to die for destiny's
seed

But still
there are those
to seek
for their want
is of this tree I speak

And it is they
to die
and it is they
to cry

For tomorrow
they shall see
but tomorrow
they will not be

For it is the greed
of absence
that feeds the tree
and they shall see
the death
they shall know
for it is all
to them the tree
shall show

But still
the serpent's tail
through time
it shall sail
To show of lands
held in the gods'
own hands

to show of places
and one thousand and ten score
faces

To show you
what shall be
and this is the quest
they see

So go ahead
and find the tree
of the dead
but don't loose your
head

For the quest
in pace
is to look death
in the face

So feed the tree
the feast
and look quick
to the beast

For tomorrow is there
forever to fare

But you'll pay the
toll
with your own soul

So fair be your
quest
for it is in
the rot of the tree
you'll rest

And there you can share
what you saw
with all

But they too
have seen the sight
of the ever knowing
light

As in the tree
they too lay
never to venture
the light of day

So I ask again
is what is there
to see
worth the souls of men

So I ask
why put on a mask
that will see all
if it leads
to an eternal fall

The gleam
of a sun beam
or
the cry of a child
The want of a
mother riled

So stay from
the tree
for tomorrow shall be
even if you need wait
to see

Twinkle of a Star

So far away is the light I seek
How can I call words that will tell
    of what I speak
For my words fall mute on virgin snow
a love, a desire, an emotion I dare not show
For it is so far to the twinkle of a star
for it is, for me, light years too far

I dare not speak of love, or roses
as I stand to watch the beams
    that dance in a multiple of poses

I stand to stare in ancient vain
Ghosts prance about to drive me sane
and catch me quick, as by heart I am slain
For it is so distant to the twinkle of a star
for it is, for me, light years too far

To hold, to be held by the silken strands
that leap through space like welcoming hands

Har'i Khan

I dream they pluck me up in grasp
   and let me breathe the power in her gasp
Far it is, so very far
   to reach the twinkle of a silent star

Can You See Me

Can you see me? — Do you see me?
Can you hear me? — Do you hear me?
Can you touch me? — Do you feel me?
   Here look at me!
And see the scars left within my flesh
so deep, so deep and cold, so riddled with time
These scars left by when I dared to love
These scars left by when I dared to care
These scars left by when I dared. . . . .
   Here listen to me!
And hear the story I can never tell
so deep, so deep and cold, so riddled with pain
These stories of when I dared to love
These stories of when I dared to care
These stories of when I dared. . . . .
   Here feel my thoughts!
And touch the flesh that covers my soul
So empty, so empty and cold,
So empty of love

So empty of care
So empty . . .
So empty . . .
So empty . . .

Each Time I Turn

Each time I turn around, you stand farther from my side
Each time I turn around, as from me you seem to hide
>Time shall come, with our final farewell
>as you shall slip from my futile spell
>and leave shattered, my mortal shell

>You'll carry-away with memories we share
>as from my soul, apart you shall tear
>with love and grace, of such elegant flair

For each time I turn around, you stand farther from my side
For each time I turn around, as from me you seem to hide
>So before you leave, into the mists embrace
>look to my eyes upon my plated face
>Then turn away and take my hand
>to dance away and leave me stand
>alone in my shadow, so cold and bare
>into your memory I'll stand and stare

For each time I turn around, you stand farther from
my side
For each time I turn around, as from me you seem to
slide

The Prisoner

I

The prisoner walks a battered path
each foot falls cold on ice,
the gallows 'waits his throat
for it, it shall entice

He steps in march
of sorrow bled,
A fire in his heart, as
his love lay with the dead

He saw her die
at arm's length away
Her eyes be closed
to the light of day

Her blood flowed black
cross the ebony blade
Her eyes grew dark, for
no effort had she made

For she beckoned the dagger

sheathed in her skin
For she welcomed the blade
and died with her sin

The gallows 'waits
the prisoner's stride
And upon its bed
he now shall subside

His mind upon the sea
of crystal diamonds clear
His mind's upon the sea
he saw only from the pier

As he looks to her
a gentle stare
She looks away
a sorrow to compare

Each step he takes
to the gallows's call
A memory of the night
in his mind does stall

Her loving eyes
her loving sight
The dagger plunged
into the night

His hands found stained
by her blood so red

The corpse of his love
lay on the floor dead

The prisoner strides forth
the gallows now cry
For by his own rope
the prisoner shall die

The gallows
so proud and strong
stands waiting, for
the prisoner's song

His gaze is out to sea
as a ship in harbor set
To rot at the pier
the journey never met

The ship in sorrow
rots at bay
Never to voyage
in light of day

For is it not better
to sink at sea
Then to rot at the end of a rope
the ocean to hold your Cree'

But the gallows grows closer
but the gallows grows cold
And from the gallows

the prisoner, a story told

For when they found his love
laying in his grip
They saw the dagger,
from his fingers slip

So now the gallows
'waits his throat
And around him now
there grows a moat

As he is sentenced
by his peers, in hate,
His trial and judgment
is sentenced by fate

For now her body
pale with deed
Lay in a crypt
a corpse of her steed

And now the prisoner
on deck does stand
One last rose drops
from his hand

To his peers he looks out
with a grief sunk heart
Their blank faces look
so cold and tart

He does not cry
but grieves the pain
As all to drive
A madman sane

II

The prisoner walks a battered path
each foot falls cold on ice
The gallows 'waits his throat
for it, it scale entice

But what of his crime
for which he's there
Set to fall
from life he'll tear

The dagger stained
found in his hand
And with the corpse
he did stand

To hold her tight
'til light of day
'til dawn to come
he'd stand to pray

But no day came
into the crypt
Just the fools

to write his script

For all they saw
were his blood stained hands
They never saw, in the corner,
another did stand

The prisoner stands
for time to wait
As with his throat
the noose shall mate

He stands so proud
draped in black
His withered body
his dreams in a sack

For now she sets
in her own little tomb
Chained to the corpse
that brought her doom

The dead man that
held the blade
As in her flesh, it was he
the incision made

And as for the prisoner
to await the noose
His heart held tight
his neck left loose

For this gallows
has no rope
And none shall hang
in its empty hope

Still for the prisoner's crime
he has to pay
And there on the gallows
he'll stand each day

But what is his crime
for what is his guilt
for what did he do
to make the balance tilt

He dared to love
He dared to care
And for her, his heart
he dared to tear

And now he stands
always wanting, never knowing
As now he stands
his pain just keeps growing

For as the ship
tied to the pier
Out to sea,
a desiring leer

For is it not better

to stand and die
Not to know the march
of a gallant try

III

The Prisoner on a battered path
each foot falls cold in ice
The gallows 'waits his throat
for it, it shall entice

As to his love
a gentle tear to fall
As in his sorrow
she doesn't hear his call

The cry of pain
the cry of sorrow
A pain as if shot
from a spiteful arrow

He now be damned
to always want
His soul by memory
will always taunt

Always wanting
never knowing
There is nothing now to stop
the pain from growing

He'll always wonder
the full of her lips
Or were they barbed
as needle-tips

He'll always wonder,
the feel of her skin
Or was it cold and hard
as if made of tin

He stands at the gallows
his sorrow there does show
Damned he is, to always wonder
but never shall he know

The warmth in her eyes
the softness in her hart
The times they would laugh
or when the tears would start

But a corpse cannot love
But a corpse cannot care
For all a corpse can do
is unjustly compare

IV

The prisoner on the gallows stands
his feet so cold in ice
His lonely throat has

no rope to entice

But his fate,
as one of two
All for love
it holds so true

His deed is done
in guilt to stand
An empty chalice
in his hand

Always wanting
never knowing
His bleeding heart
is now showing

And now she sets
in her own tomb
By case of the sorrow
cast in her own gloom

For by her side
her murderer is laid
A corpse, in its vane
her pain was made

Shacked to his corpse
in silence she does cry
For the prisoner
she shall always despise

Both held in pain
both standing slain

Her love for the corpse
is her death's embrace
Her death is the,
prisoner's final grace.

Last Man Standing

I am the first here
    before they come
    We wait

I am the one to set things ready
    for when they come
    We wait

I know he's here with me . . . . watching
    for them to come
    We wait

The cars arrive one by one
    as they come
    We wait

They stand and say their prayers
    and whisper memories
    We wait

I stand back and watch them
    death beside me
    We wait

They leave . . . back to their cars . . .
    Back to their lives
    We wait

I am the one to close the event at hand
    and fill the grave that I dug
    No more do we wait

As I put to rest this life we now share
    in final scene and curtain call
    Now that we have spent an eternity
    together

Ancient Infant

So cold is the voice of the child lost
for to the fire was by its parents tossed

Now here in empty halls the ancient infant cries
As once it called from in its cradle where it lies

So long ago was its birth from mother's womb
So soon shall come its silk lined tomb

What years have been seen by this aged soul?
Why does it lie and wait for death to fill its bowl?

So long ago in mother's grasp it did lay
Now its children bring life into the light of day

Now here in the empty hall I have come
to hear the crying of an infant
That has seen so many days in final sum

    Good night days of past enlightenment
    as unto death you now are to be sent
      by the youth of your descent

Why do I dare

I dared to touch, I reached to care
and now I set with an emptied stare
    I look to a star, a beauty uncompared
    and found within such brilliance flared

I dared to look, I reached too far
and now I set to wish on a distant star
    I look to that star, so hidden by mist
    and remember that star I reached out and
    kissed

I dared to stare into her gaze
and watched her wander off, into a haze
    I look through the mist in queried daze
    and find I stand in a haunted maze

I dared to feel, I dared to love
and now I wait for the return of the dove
    Her gentle touch, her sweetest word
    through my soul, a wish is stirred

I listen and I wait, I reached out to care
and now I sit with a hopeful stare

As I to dream upon that star
that wasn't always so distant and far

Tear drop

In a dream of time afar
I set in a room with a wondrous star
    She glistened and shined with a light of
    despair
    as from this star I could not tear
        So tight in her grasp
        I inhaled her gasp

No walls did march this room
so dark and bleak as if a tomb
    There from her eye, a tear did fall
    and on to the air, a whisper I heard call
        So tight in her grasp
        I inhaled her gasp

Together we played, I and this tear
it shined so bright, as a well polished mirror
        Then into the clouds
    our souls ascended away from the crowds
        So tight in her grasp
            I inhaled her gasp

In the plotter's field, I pronounced my love
as it was returned by this black feathered dove
 We danced and we played as we rolled
 round the floor
 for every moment that passed we cried for
 two more
  So tight in her grasp
  I inhaled her gasp

 Then the room grew smaller
 and the tear grew older
 the room fell away
 and the light grew bolder

Till where was the tear that once played in the
night
now stood a woman bold in the light
 Now I stood in a mist of steam
 still caught in the night of the dream
  wanting to hold her grasp
  wishing to taste her gasp

 Then with a final kiss
 tragedy stung my heart's break
 For the woman in my dream
 from her sleep I saw her wake

And now here I stand alone
in a dream that we made
looking so cold in the night
where once together we had laid

Contact Har' i Khan at
poet767@msn.com
or order more copies of this book at

Tate Publishing, LLC

127 East Trade Center Terrace
Mustang, Oklahoma 73064

(888) 361 - 9473

Tate Publishing, LLC
www.tatepublishing.com